Animals
of Australia

LEVEL 2 READER

Illustrated by Edizioni Larus S.p.A.

Printed in China

KOALA

CASSOWARY

WALLABY

TASMANIAN
DEVIL

NUMBAT

ECHIDNA

Australia is filled with animals that are very, very different from animals in other lands. There are many birds, mammals, reptiles, and *marsupials* (mar-SOO-pee-uhls). A marsupial carries its baby in a pouch on its body.

KANGAROO

COCKATOO

AUSTRALIAN PHEASANT

MARSUPIAL RAT

THORNY DEVIL

Koala

The koala looks like a teddy, but it's a marsupial—*not* a bear! It has very strong, sharp toenails that cling tightly to branches. Koalas spend most of their time in the trees and only eat eucalyptus (you-kuh-LIP-tus) leaves.

A baby koala
is called a joey.
A newborn joey
is about the size
of a lima bean.
It lives in its
mother's pouch for
about six months.
Young joeys also
ride around on their
mother's back.

Red Kangaroo

Kangaroos are the world's biggest marsupials. When the red kangaroo stands up, it's taller than a man! Kangaroos like very dry areas. They eat plants and fresh grass. Those long legs help them jump, jump, jump! "Big reds" can "long jump" up to 17 feet!

A baby kangaroo is called a joey. A newborn joey is pink with no hair. It lives in its mother's pouch until it can hop about on its own.

Kangaroos can box. A male can even "stand" on its tail and kickbox!

The wallaby is like a small kangaroo. It is an excellent jumper! It hops around dry rocky places, looking for roots, leaves, and grass to eat. Wallaby joeys must keep up with their mothers.

A sugar glider is a marsupial that looks like a small gray opossum. It has a special way of getting from branch to branch. It has wide flaps of skin between its front and back feet. It spreads these out and glides. It has its own parachute!

Platypus

The platypus (PLAT-i-pus) is an odd-looking animal. It has webbed feet like an otter, a beak like a duck, and a tail like a beaver. It is a mammal—but it lays eggs! It lives in rivers and is a good swimmer. It eats shrimp, worms, insects, and small fish.

Echidna

The echidna (eh-KID-nuh) is also called a spiny anteater. It is covered with sharp prickles. Don't touch!

The echidna hunts at night. It catches ants, termites, and worms with its sticky tongue. A baby echidna is called a puggle.

Wombat

The shy wombat is a "cousin" to the koala. It eats grass, roots, and leaves. It has very strong nails that it uses to dig tunnels and a den. It uses its own body to block the den, so no other animal can get in.

Numbat

The numbat is a marsupial, but it does not have a pouch. Baby numbats hang on tightly to their mother's belly fur whenever she moves.

The numbat has a bushy tail and a long, sticky tongue that's good for catching insects. It can gobble up thousands of termites in one day!

The little bilby (BILL-bee) has a pointy nose that can sniff out insects. It looks like a rabbit and lives in an underground den. Baby bilbies stay in their mother's pouch until they can prance about on their own. A bilby is also called a bandicoot and a pinkie. It likes to eat termites. Yum!

Kookaburra

The kookaburra (COOK-ah-burr-ah) is a big bird about 15 inches long. Look at its big head! Its big beak helps it catch large bugs, small birds, mice, lizards—and it loves snakes! It builds a nest in a hollow tree trunk.

At sunrise, the kookaburra lets out a loud "laugh" that wakes everybody up. It's like an alarm clock!

Emu

The emu (EE-myu) is a huge bird. It stands higher than a man and weighs more than 100 pounds. It can't fly, but it can run as fast as a horse!

A mother emu digs a hole in the ground to lay her eggs in. Then the father emu takes care of the eggs.

Cassowary

The cassowary (CASS-o-wahr-ee) is also a big bird. It has wings with prickly feathers. It cannot fly, but it is a good jumper and swimmer. Cassowaries eat grass, leaves, seeds, worms, and bugs. Mother cassowaries lay eggs in a nest of leaves, and the father sits on the eggs to keep them warm until they hatch.

Dingo

Dingoes are wild dogs that live in small packs. They move from place to place, and are fast runners. They hunt animals of all sizes—kangaroos, wallabies, wombats, sheep, and rats. Dingoes don't bark. They howl, like wolves.

A mother dingo makes a den near water. The babies are called pups.

The Tasmanian (Taz-MAIN-ee-uhn) devil is a fierce animal with sharp claws and teeth. It has a loud scream. And it smells just awful when it is afraid! It lives on the Australian island state of Tasmania.

In the day, it rests in its den. At night, it hunts wallabies, rats, birds, lizards, and fish.

King Brown Snake

Australia has more poisonous snakes than any other place on Earth. The king brown snake (also called a mulga) can be 9 feet long! It is one of the largest poisonous snakes in Australia. A bite from the king brown snake is dangerous. Its fangs are longer than an inch!

Frill-Necked Lizard

Look at the frill on the neck of this lizard! When this "frilled dragon" meets an enemy, it hisses and fans out its frill like an umbrella! This scares its enemy and gives the lizard time to escape. It eats insects, spiders, small mammals, and bird eggs.

Johnston's Crocodile

Johnston's crocodile is a shy croc that lives in rivers and ponds. It's about 7 feet long and does not hurt people. It would rather eat fish.

Marine Crocodile

The biggest and most dangerous croc is the marine crocodile. It can grow up to 30 feet long! It lives in rivers and swamps. It can also swim from island to island in saltwater. It is sometimes called a "saltie."

This huge croc eats fish, crabs, and mammals—even big mammals. It can leap at them—from right out of the water! Stay away!

Cockatoo

Cockatoos live in forests and sometimes in big city parks. There are many different kinds, and all are beautiful, smart birds. They can live for 40 to 50 years and are often kept as pets.

GALAH

SULFUR-CRESTED COCKATOO

Some cockatoos can copy the sounds they hear and even "talk" like people. G'day, mate!